AF406680

Latter-day Grooks

From the Words & Wisdom of

Russell M. Nelson

Bill Wylson

Available at:
billwylsonbooks.com

Author's Note: The grooks presented in this work are taken from the writings and teachings of Russell M. Nelson, Prophet and President of The Church of Jesus Christ of Latter-day Saints. I have attempted to cite sources from the published writings of President Nelson; however, I have no authority or commission to speak in any official capacity for President Nelson or for the Church.

The ideas expressed herein represent nothing more than the opinion of the author.

First Edition published July 2022
Second Edition published March 2024

Green Stem Media
White Horse Books
Salt Lake City, Utah 84009

Table of Contents

A Brief Introduction to Grooks

What is a Grook?

Many have tried to define what a grook essentially is. Most grooks say what many of us think, but they put pertinent new perspectives on everyday observations, presenting the reader with small instructions in the art of living.

A grook, (or 'gruk' in the Danish language) is a short aphoristic poem. Grooks were initially created by the Danish poet Piet Hein (1905–1996), who wrote over 10,000 of them in Danish and English. Grooks capture profound meaning in a few simple lines. The beauty of grooks lies not only in their brevity but also in how they embody wisdom and profound cultural truths. Through simple yet resonant language, grooks make readers deeply contemplate life's various themes and experiences.

What is a Latter-day Grook?

As Latter-day Saints, we have a distinctive collection of wisdom and insight that remains primarily unacquainted to the outside world. This literature houses profound wisdom concerning life's most significant existential questions. It addresses themes like morality, righteousness, faith, and divinity. The revealed knowledge present within our literature is deeply rooted in our theology.

It is often easier to recall essential writings when they appear in poetic form because poetry resonates with us. We enjoy reading or hearing something that reflects what is in our minds or hearts. The message of these Latter-day Grooks can be inscribed in our hearts and minds and offer us hope, strength, and encouragement in our effort to resist evil and overcome the world.

Catch the Wave

A wonderous wave
of righteous truth,
spreads from ridge to rim,

empowered by
seven simple words:

"This is my Beloved
Son…Hear Him."

Roots

We all
are the work
of our Creator's hand;

roots of
divinity—imbedded
in mortal land.

0,79€
1,15€
2,54€
1,50€
2,20€
1,9
1,90€
1,69€

Spiritual Shortages

The success
of the worldly

is a hollow ache—
when we mistake

living well
for living worthily.

HIGH ROAD
LOW ROAD

Choices

Let your unique
identity shape
each vital decision
that you make,

remembering and knowing:

> Who you are,
> why you are here,
> and where you are
> going.

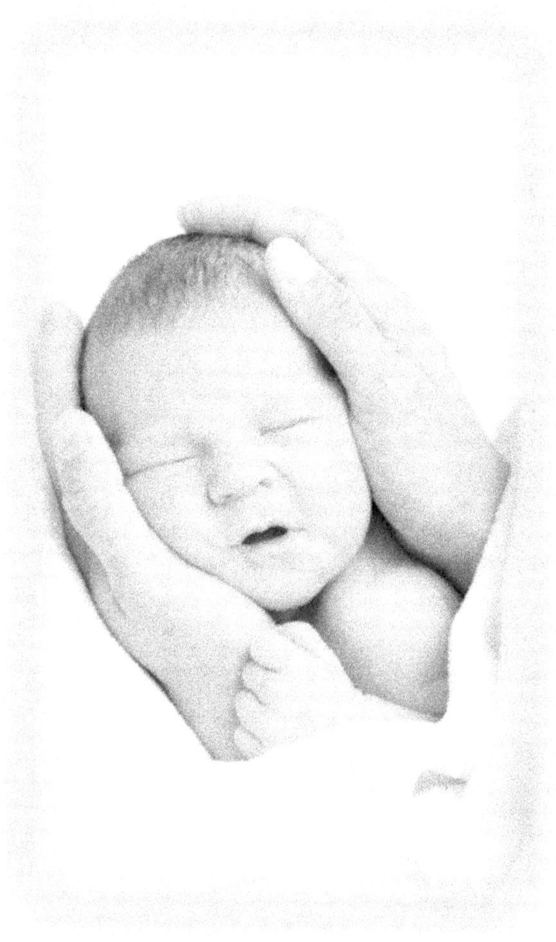

Who You Are

One of God's great
and noble spirits,
held in reserve
for this time of need.

One of the Covenant,
heir to the promise
that all earth will be blessed
through Abraham's seed.

Chapter 1
Where do we begin?

Why You Are Here

To exercise agency
that divine gift to you—

to freely choose

>who you will be
>and what you will do.

Where You Are Going

With each passing sunset,
we are closer to judgment

for our intents, our desires
and all that we've done.

It's a simple matter
of a life hereafter

in the glory of the stars,
the moon, or the sun.

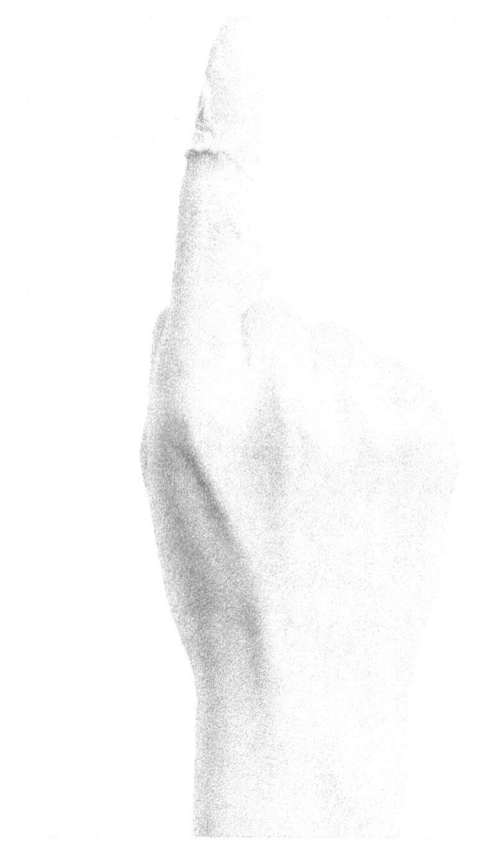

Bright Recollection

Your everyday thoughts
have not been lost.
The mind will present

perfect remembrance
at the moment
of divine judgment.

A Gospel of Change

When we discern
eternity's range

we are never
        too young to learn,

and never
        too old to change.

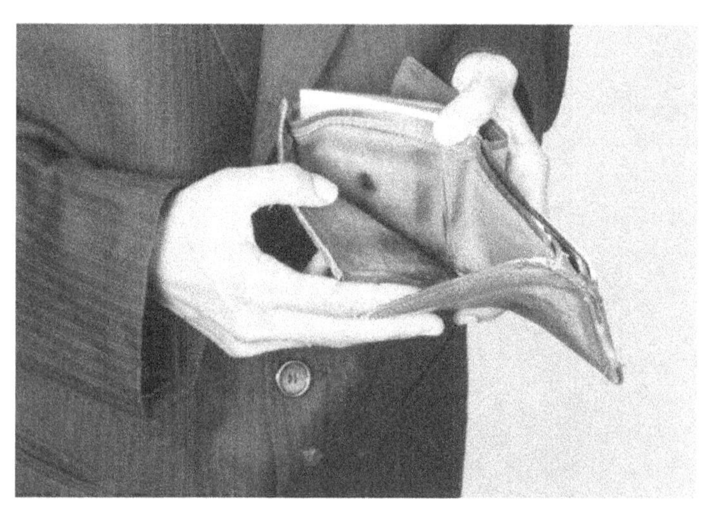

Something a Little More Filling

Affluence is empty—
when accompanied by
spiritual privation.

And hunger persists—
when the spirit itself
is subject to starvation.

Dying, We Live

Born to die
we die to live.
The doors of death,
they beckon.

As seedlings of God
we barely blossom on earth
yet fully flower
in heaven.

A Time to Die

*"It was not expedient that man should be
reclaimed from this temporal death."* (Alma 42:8)

If all sixty-nine billion
of Earth's continuous
demographic

remained on this planet,
well, just imagine
the traffic!

The Pathway to Purity

The key to avoiding misery
inflicted by the adversary

is a process, not an event:

Repent!

    Repent!

        Repent!

BE THE BEST
VERSION OF YOU

The Joy of Redemption

Many consider
repentance a punishment,

to be avoided
at all cost or exertion.

But when we change,
and choose to repent,

the Savior transforms us
into our very best version.

Greater Worth

If you were offered
diamonds or rubies,
in sparkling, dazzling hues

or

the Book of Mormon,
honestly,
which would you choose?

Which *is* of greater
worth to you?

Unfinished Business

Today I have
a little more time

to be perhaps
a little more kind,

quicker to thank,
slower to scold,

more generous in sharing,
more gracious in caring,

to live life well
with potential untold.

Moving Along the Path

Whether you are
diligently moving

along, or have slipped
or stepped away—

experience the strength
of being and doing

a little bit better each day.

The Battle

Do better. Be better
because the battle
with sin is real.

The enemy arms his minions
with potent, powerful weapons

to destroy
all the joy
we could feel.

Making Time

The voices of the world—
engaging, deceptive, seductive,
can pull us off the

         covenant path.

But counter their lure—
making time for the Lord
and avoid their inevitable

         aftermath.

A Steady Beat

Without daily prayer
and continuous
gospel review,

we are vulnerable
to philosophies
intriguing but untrue.

Even Saints
who are faithful
still often can

be derailed by
the steady beat
of Babylon's band.

An Invitation

"The gospel of Jesus Christ is a gospel of repentance."

Keep changing,
and growing,
and becoming more pure.

Through His Gift—
hope, healing,
and progress endure!

Spiritual Foundation

When facing upheaval
or similar unsettling events,
        the safest place to be
        spiritually
is living *inside* temple covenants.

A Message of Joy

Our spirits
rejoice

with every
right choice

      we make,

and with every
small, forward step

      we take.

Better Than Ever

What stands in your
way of repentance?
What stops you from
entering that door?

We can change and repent
      and do better—
      be better
than ever before.

Gathering Israel

The charge for us is
to be *worthy* and *willing*

to prepare the world
for Christ's Second Coming.

A Holy Place

In this world, as
faith and holiness
decrease,

our need for holy places
will constantly
increase.

Continue to make
(with increased pace)

your home a truly
holy place.

Believe

The Lord does not require
perfect faith for us
to receive

access to His *perfect* power.
But He does ask us
to believe.

Increase Your Faith

Start today
and do your best,

and Christ will increase
your adeptness

at moving mountains
as large as Everest.

Faith Takes Work

Lazy learners and
lax disciples

always struggle
but barely muster

the faith of even
A grain of mustard.

It Takes Faith

It takes faith
to join the Church
and remain eternally true.

It takes faith
to follow prophets over
pundits or popular view.

It takes faith
to serve a mission in a world with
values misplaced.

It takes faith
when friends oppose us,
to live a life that's chaste.

It takes faith
to teach the gospel
to children not fully grown.

So, never ever minimize
the amount of faith
you already own.

He Will Never Fail

If everything
and everyone
you trust in this world
should fail,

Jesus Christ's
love for you
will everlastingly
prevail.

He never slumbers;
never sleeps.
All promises and covenants
He keeps.

He has overcome all sorrow.
He works miracles today
and He'll work His miracles

tomorrow.

Are You Ready?

Will you
let His will
take precedence
over every other

type of ambition?

Will you
let your will
succumb to His?
Are you ready for

that type of submission?

Look Forward

We live in a glorious
age and dispensation.

No spiritual blessing will be
withheld from this generation.

Despite the world's
constant commotion—

We look forward to the future
"with joyful anticipation."

Move Forward

Don't spin your wheels
in memories of yesterday.

The gathering of Israel
moves forward today.

The Lord directs His Church,
it's purposes providential.

Our challenge is to achieve (someday)
our own divine potential.

NEW
NORMAL

A New Normal

If you want to embrace
a new normal,
turn your heart, mind,
and soul to your Father.

Be pure in thought,
and word, and deed,
magnify callings, minister
to those in need,

always keep an
eternal perspective,
make daily repentance
a prime directive,

and prepare to meet your God.
Let that be *your* new normal.

"Hear Him!"

The admonition
given to Joseph
is also meant
for each of us.

We are to seek,
in every way,
to hear what Jesus
has to say.

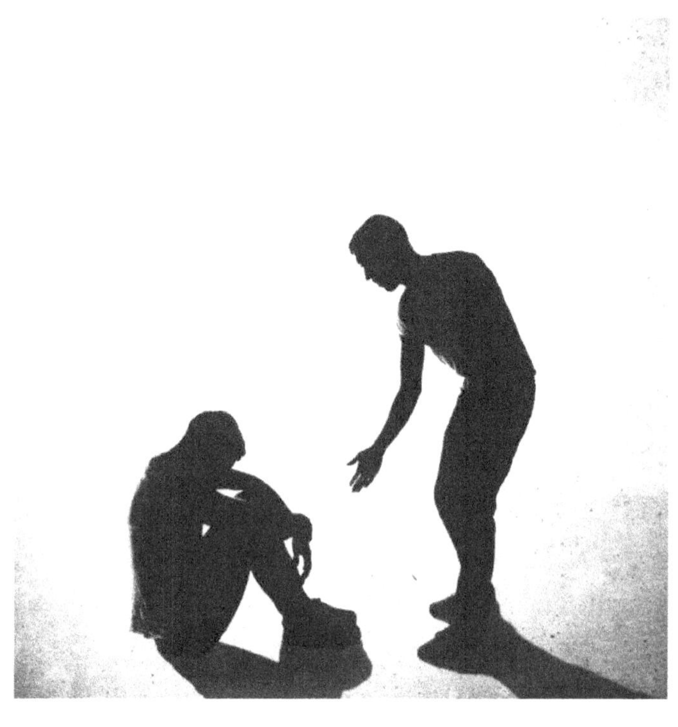

Hallmark

A hallmark of the Lord's
true and living Church
will always be

an organized and directed
effort to minister to
all of God's great family.

The Priesthood of God

We can
open locked doors,
strengthen testimonies,
heal hearts' sores.

We can
lift burdens borne,
give priesthood blessings,
save lives wayworn.

We can
spread joy abroad—
all because we hold

the Priesthood of God.

This is Our Charge

Think of your duty
as God's mighty army

to prepare the world
for the Second Coming.

This is our privilege.
This is our charge:

To share the gospel
with the world at large.

Witness

Taking upon us
the Savior's name

entails we witness
and proclaim

through our actions
and through our word—

that Jesus is
our Christ and Lord.

Sacrifice

Assaults of the adversary
increase exponentially,
in both variety
And in intensity,

But the Lord will bring you
all your needed miracles
as you sacrifice to serve
in His Holy Temples.

Riveted

"Our focus must be riveted on the Savior and His gospel."

It is rigorous—
          mentally
to look to Him—
          unlimitedly
in every thought and deed.

But when our focus
          assuredly
is riveted
          securely

all doubts and fears will flee.

Gasping for Air

Reach up
with all the intensity
of a drowning soul grasping
and gasping for air,

and when
you do, the pure power
of our Lord Jesus Christ
will be there.

FOCUS
25

Focus

When we focus
our lives
on Jesus Christ,

we can feel gladness

regardless of
what is—or isn't
happening—

in this world of madness.

The Source

The joy that we feel
has little to deal
            with circumstance

and everything to do
with the focus and view
        of our glance.

Joy comes from and
because of Him:
Its one true source
            and only substance.

Brimming with Joy

Joy brings God's power into our lives.
The cross was endured by Jesus Christ

"for the joy that was set before Him."

Think on that! Our Savior endured
the most excruciating pain on earth,

yet His joy was filled to the brim.

Focus on Joy

What will be possible
        after repenting?
What weakness will
        become strength?

What chastening will
        convert to blessing?
What tragedy will turn
        to good at length?

        We, too, can endure
        every challenging service
        as we focus on the joy
        the Lord "set before" us?

        .

A Priceless Possession

Every day that we
keep our covenants
and try to live
by celestial laws,

and every day that we
help others in that
self-same,
glorious cause,

joy will be ours.

Settlers

"I fear that too many have sadly surrendered their agency to the adversary."

Why would anyone settle
for Esau's mess of pottage

who has been promised all
the blessings of Abraham's cottage?

Pray from the Heart

"The Lord will teach you."

Polite recitations
punctuated with petitions
cannot constitute
communing with God.

Are you willing to pray—
hour-by hour—
to learn *how* to pray
for God's lasting power?

WHILE YOU TEACH
YOU LEARN

The Lord's Way

"I give unto you a commandment that you shall teach one another the doctrine of the kingdom."

The Lord's way of helping you
comprehend the gospel's core

is this:

As you *teach* the gospel,
you will learn even more.

Let It Show

Day after day,
as along the pathway
toward eternal destiny you go—

Increase your faith!

Proclaim your faith!

And simply allow
your faith to show!

Truth is Truth

"Truth is truth! It is not divisible, and any part of it cannot be set aside."

Whether truth emerges abroad
from scientific elaboration
or through divine revelation,
all truth emanates from God.

All truth—
no matter how it is sliced—
is part and parcel
of the gospel of Christ.

Naturally

The natural outcome
of one's conversion,
worthiness,
preparation,
and gospel submersion

is—on an
exponential curve—
a stronger
and stronger
desire to serve.

Kudos

The greatest
compliment

that can be earned,
given, or lent,

is simple and goes
no deeper

than to be known
as a true covenant keeper.

Unfailing Faith

Unfailing faith
is fortified
through heartfelt
and sincere prayer.

God will strengthen
your steady faith
truly
beyond compare.

Plague

"One of the plagues of our day is that too few people know where to turn for truth."

Never in history
has there been such a moment

when the knowledge of our Savior

has been more personally
vital and relevant

to every human soul's behavior.

His Power

As we keep our temple covenants,
with His power we are fed.

And oh, how we'll need His power
in the coming days ahead.

A Vital Message

"The gospel of Jesus Christ is exactly what is needed in this confused, contentious, and weary world."

Each child of God
deserves to hear
the redeeming message
of Jesus our Savior.

No pronouncement is
more vital or dear
to our hope and happiness
now and forever.

We Show Our Love by Serving

If you know someone
alone and blue,

reach out—

even if you feel
all alone too!

You don't need a reason
or message to speak of—

Just say hello
and show
your love.

A Brief History of Grooks

Grooks were originally created by the Danish poet Piet Hein, (1905–1996) who wrote over 10,000 of them in both the Danish and English languages. Hein was a polymath (designer, mathematician, inventor, author, and poet), often writing under the pseudonym Kumbel, meaning 'tombstone.'

A grook ('gruk' in Danish) is a short aphoristic poem or rhyming aphorism. Aphorisms are concise, terse, laconic, or memorable expressions of a general truth or principle. They are often handed down by tradition from generation to generation. Literary experts suggest that the term 'gruk' is a compilation of the Danish words 'GRin and sUK', meaning to laugh and sigh, but Piet Hein said he felt that the word came to him out of thin air.

Aphoristic collections, known as wisdom literature, are prominent in Western civilization. They have had a profound impact on the canons of ancient societies, such as the literature of Hinduism and Buddhism, the Biblical Ecclesiastes, Islamic hadiths, the golden verses of Pythagoras, Hesiod's Works and Days, the Delphic maxims, and Epictetus'

Handbook. A 1559 oil–on–oak-panel painting, Netherlandish Proverbs (also called The Blue Cloak or The Topsy Turvy World) by Pieter Bruegel, the Elder, artfully depicts a land populated with literal renditions of Flemish aphorisms of the day.

Hein, a direct descendant of Piet Pieterszoon Hein, the 17th century Dutch naval hero, was born in Copenhagen, Denmark. He studied at the Institute for Theoretical Physics of the University of Copenhagen (later to become the Niels Bohr Institute), and Technical University of Denmark. Yale awarded him an honorary doctorate in 1972. When the Germans first occupied Denmark, Piet Hein was confronted with a dilemma. He felt he had three choices; do nothing, flee to neutral Sweden, or join the Danish resistance movement. As he explained in 1968:

"Sweden was out because I am not Swedish, but Danish. I could not remain at home because, if I had, every knock at the door would have sent shivers up my spine. So, I joined the Resistance."

Hein's greatest weapon was his pen. Hein's short poems, or gruks, first appeared in the daily newspaper *Politiken* in April 1940 shortly after the German occupation of Denmark. His grooks were meant to be a spirit-building, coded form of passive resistance. The grooks are multi-faceted and characterized by irony, paradox, brevity, precise use of language, rhythm, and rhyme. They were often satiric in nature.

Hein's first grook passed the Nazi censors who did not grasp its true, hidden meaning:

CONSOLATION GROOK

Losing one glove
is certainly painful,
but nothing
compared to the pain
of losing one,
throwing away the other,
and finding
the first one again.

The Danes understood the deeper meaning and importance of Hein's grook and graffitied it all over the country. The hidden message was that even if you lose your freedom (i.e., losing one glove), do not lose your patriotism and self-respect by collaborating with the Nazis ('throwing away the other glove'), because betraying your country would be more painful when freedom had been won again.

Latter-day Saints are in a type of resistance movement of our own. We are fighting the forces of evil and resisting the temptations of Satan and the world. It would be tragic indeed if we lost our faith in a moment of crisis and threw away the blessings of eternity promised to the faithful. Faith in Jesus Christ will always be rewarded.

It is my sincere prayer that the messages of these Latter-day Grooks will be graffitied onto the walls of our hearts and minds and offer us hope, strength, and encouragement in our effort to resist evil and overcome the world.

"Keep thy father's commandment, and forsake not the law of thy mother:

"Bind them continually upon thine heart, and tie them about thy neck.

"When thou goest, it shall lead thee; when thou sleepest, it shall keep thee; and when thou awakest, it shall talk with thee."

Proverbs 6: 20-22

About the Author

Bill Wylson is the author of over 55 published writings dealing with family values, religious issues and religious education. His work has appeared in *The Ensign, This People, The New Era, Liberty Magazine, Success,* and others.

Bill graduated from the *Columbia School of Broadcasting* in Hollywood, CA as a commercial copywriter. He wrote trade journal ads for a major advertising agency in Los Angeles and public service announcements for a Los Angeles television station.

In addition to his church callings, he has served as a volunteer Board Member of *Advocates of Single Parent Youth, Special Fun Games for the Disabled,* and on the Boards of Arts and Theater Councils. He has also served on Advisory Committees for the *Volunteer Center of Los Angeles* and on the *United Way Government Affairs Committee.*

Bill Wylson currently lives in South Jordan, Utah.

References

A Gospel of Change	Gen. Conf. October 2013
A Holy Place	Gen. Conf. April 2021
A Message of Joy	Gen. Conf. April 2021
A New Normal	Gen. Conf. October 2020
A Priceless Possession	Gen Conf. October 2016
A Time to Die	Gen. Conf. April 1992
A Vital Message	Gen. Conf. April 2021
An Invitation	Gen. Conf. April 2021
Are You Ready?	Gen. Conf. October 2020
Believe	Gen. Conf. April 2021
Better Than Ever	Ensign, January 2015
Bright Recollection	Gen. Conf. October 1990
Brimming with Joy	Gen. Conf. October 2016
Catch the Wave	Gen. Conf. April 2013
Choices	Gen. Conf. October 1990
Dying, We Live	Gen. Conf. April 1992
Faith Takes Work	Gen. Conf. April 2021
Focus	Gen. Conf. October 2016
Focus on Joy	Gen. Conf. October 2016
Gasping for Air	Gen. Conf. April 2017
Gathering Israel	Gen. Conf. April 2021
Greater Worth	Gen. Conf. October 2017
Hallmark	Gen. Conf. April 2018
"Hear Him"	Gen. Conf. April 2020
He Will Never Fail	Gen. Conf. April 2021
His Power	Gen. Conf. October 2021
Increase Your Faith	Gen. Conf. April 2021
It Takes Faith	Gen. Conf. April 2021
Kudos	Gen. Conf. October 2011
Let It Show	Gen. Conf. October 2013
Look Forward	Gen. Conf. October 2020
Making Time	Gen. Conf. October 2021
Move Forward	Gen. Conf. October 2020
Moving Along the Path	Gen. Conf. April 2019
Naturally	Gen. Conf. October 2012

Plague	Gen. Conf. October 2021
Pray from the Heart	Gen. Conf. April 2016
Riveted	Gen. Conf. April 2017
Roots	Gen. Conf. April 2004
Sacrifice	Gen. Conf. October 2018
Settlers	Gen. Conf. April 2016
Something a Little More Filling	Gen. Conf. April 1996
Spiritual Foundation	Gen. Conf. October 2021
Spiritual Shortages	Gen. Conf. April 1996
Steady Beat	Gen. Conf. October 2021
The Battle	Ensign, January 2015
The Joy of Redemption	Gen. Conf. April 2019
The Lord's Way	Gen. Conf. April 2015
The Pathway to Purity	Gen. Conf. April 2019
The Priesthood of God	Gen. Conf. April 2018
The Source	Gen. Conf. October 2016
This is Our Charge	Gen. Conf. April 2018
Truth is Truth!	Gen. Conf. April 2014
Unfailing Faith	Gen. Conf. April 2011
Unfinished Business	Gen. Conf. April 1992
We Show Our Love By Serving	Gen. Conf. April 2021
Where You Are Going	Gen. Conf. October 1990
Who You Are	Gen. Conf. October 1990
Why You Are Here	Gen. Conf. October 1990
Witness	Gen. Conf. April 2020

www.ingramcontent.com/pod-product-compliance
Lightning Source LLC
Chambersburg PA
CBHW071318130726
47996CB00002B/532